HAMILTON

FRANK KEATING

PAINTINGS BY

MIKE WIMMER

A Paula Wiseman Book

SIMON & SCHUSTER BOOKS FOR YOUNG READERS

NEW YORK   LONDON   TORONTO   SYDNEY   NEW DELHI

All quotes used in this book are accurate and attributed to Alexander Hamilton.

The illustrator gratefully acknowledges everyone at Colonial Williamsburg who keeps history alive and who helped with the research for this book. And in addition, grateful acknowledgment to Catherine Whittenburg for her generosity and patience in helping to bring authenticity and historical accuracy to these pages.

SIMON & SCHUSTER BOOKS FOR YOUNG READERS

An imprint of Simon & Schuster Children's Publishing Division

1230 Avenue of the Americas, New York, New York 10020

Text copyright © 2020 by Frank Keating

Illustrations copyright © 2020 by Mike Wimmer

All rights reserved, including the right of reproduction in whole or in part in any form.

SIMON & SCHUSTER BOOKS FOR YOUNG READERS is a trademark of Simon & Schuster, Inc.

For information about special discounts for bulk purchases, please contact Simon & Schuster

Special Sales at 1-866-506-1949 or business@simonandschuster.com.

The Simon & Schuster Speakers Bureau can bring authors to your live event.

For more information or to book an event, contact the Simon & Schuster Speakers Bureau

at 1-866-248-3049 or visit our website at www.simonspeakers.com.

Book design by Tom Daly

The text for this book was set in Adobe Caslon Pro.

The illustrations for this book were rendered in oil on canvas.

Manufactured in China

0720 SCP

First Edition

10 9 8 7 6 5 4 3 2 1

Library of Congress Cataloging-in-Publication Data

Names: Keating, Francis Anthony, 1944– author. | Wimmer, Mike, illustrator.

Title: Hamilton / Frank Keating ; illustrated by Mike Wimmer.

Description: New York : Simon & Schuster Books for Young Readers, [2020] |

Audience: Ages 4–8 | Audience: Grades 2–3 | Summary: "A picture book biography of

Alexander Hamilton's life from boyhood to becoming a Founding Father."— Provided by publisher.

Identifiers: LCCN 2019052790 (print) | LCCN 2019052791 (eBook) |

ISBN 9781534406568 (hardback) | ISBN 9781534406575 (eBook)

Subjects: LCSH: Hamilton, Alexander, 1757–1804—Juvenile literature. | Statesmen—United States—

Biography—Juvenile literature. | United States—Politics and government—1783–1809—Juvenile literature.

Classification: LCC E302.6.H2 K43 2020 (print) | LCC E302.6.H2 (eBook) |

DDC 973.4092 [B]—dc23

LC record available at https://lccn.loc.gov/2019052790

LC eBook record available at https://lccn.loc.gov/2019052791

America's extraordinary story was first told by its founders. To proclaim independence and to face and defeat the greatest military power of the age was extraordinary. All from an idea. Our founders sacrificed everything for liberty. This book is dedicated to those long-dead, courageous souls.

—F. K.

I want to dedicate this book to all those born out of privilege who create their own opportunities through hard work, dedication to education, and the ability to reinvent themselves after failure.

—M. W.

I was a Father of my country. I was there when we became a free and sovereign nation. Not more than a boy, I wrote pamphlets supporting the cause of liberty. I spoke in the streets. Though we were a colony, I said that all men have a right to govern themselves.

"The sacred rights of mankind . . . are written, as with a sunbeam . . . by the hand of the divinity itself."

I argued. I wrote. I was at the center, the passion and fire, of the creation of a new land.

But my life was not expected to be that way.

I was born on January 11, 1755. Not in America, but in a small town on the island of Nevis in the West Indies. In the Caribbean, where I gloried in the smell of cinnamon, nutmeg, avocado, and ginger root. Around me was the sea, and on the land were whirring windmills that crushed sugarcane, the principal crop of my island home. My friends and I hiked through fields and scenes sprinkled with smells of yams, sweet potatoes, smoked ham, and fresh fish. Everywhere were the colorful and wild aloe vera plants, a common sight in the tropics.

As a child, I attended a small Hebrew school, though I was largely homeschooled. My mother taught me French. She also taught me the Ten Commandments. I was small and frequently was placed on a table to stand and recite.

When I was ten years old, we moved to Saint Croix, another island in the Caribbean.

My mother became a shopkeeper and I became a part-time clerk. We kept a goat for milk. I minded the store and kept the books and watched the inventory.

And then my happiness ended. My mother died.
My brother and I were orphaned and penniless.

I lived as I could. At age twelve, I was on my own. I began
to read, and read all that I could from the small library that
my mother left me. Alexander Pope. Plutarch. I learned math
and chemistry. I learned about money and marketing. I began
to write poetry. I also learned that I would rise in the world
only through education and hard work. I read. And learned.
And worked. I was noticed by leading businessmen on Saint
Croix, who raised the money to permit me to complete my
education. I sailed to America, never to return
to the Caribbean.

I was seventeen.

I settled in New York City and became a college student. I studied the Bible. I also studied geography, literature, speech, Greek, and Latin. I also plunged into the debates that roiled the land. We may be British colonies but we have the rights of Englishmen. Shall we be free or shall a faraway land tell us what to do? I argued that no law was just without the will of the people. I wrote essays. I raced through my studies and pursued the cause of liberty. I was all action.

"I cannot make everyone as rapid as myself." Few worked as hard as I.

I was a whirlwind.

The revolution began. Clash and combat. A war between colony and mother country. For the rights of all people. For independence. I was still young, without family or fortune.

"I am a stranger in the country. I have no property here, no connections."

I was a private in a New York militia company.

I was the captain of an artillery company.

I was a lieutenant colonel on the staff of General George Washington.

I was the "Little Lion." "Ham" or "Hammie" to my friends. I fought the enemy and was indifferent to danger. I became a war hero.

The war ended. The revolution was won. It was now time to build a nation.

But how to do it? We were young and poor, divided by thirteen different state governments and thirteen different systems of law. I became a lawyer and soon was a member of the New York Assembly and a member of the congress of the states. I argued for a strong national government with the power to tax. The government had little money to pay its bills. The country needed a standing army, a navy, a coast guard. The strength to protect its people. And money that was more than worthless paper.

"Power without revenue . . . is a bubble."

I quickly set to work. Vigor and action from me. Vigor and action for a new government. In 1789, I was still in my early thirties. I was the leading voice to call for a convention of the states to give a national congress and a national government all powers that relate to war, peace, trade, and a national currency. I argued for the creation of a national bank that would take deposits and loan money to the government to fund warships, roads, bridges, and canals. All the national needs of a strong and proud people.

"There is no time for a wrong decision. These days must be the last stage of national humiliation."

Beginning in 1787, I wrote most of the Federalist Papers, which made the argument for a strong government with three strong branches, including a strong president and an independent court system.

The states agreed, and today's government was formed.

"It's not tyranny we desire; it's a just, limited federal government."

Some of my joyous New York neighbors even called for my city to be renamed "Hamiltoniana."

The man whom I admired above all others, George Washington, became the first president of the United States. He asked me to be the first secretary of the treasury. I had the vision and the energy to right the government's finances. I set the dollar as the national currency. I formed the Customs Service. I encouraged the creation of banks so that commerce would flourish.

"Men give me credit for some genius. All the genius I have lies in this: when I have a subject in hand, I study it profoundly. Day and night it is before me.
It is the fruit of labor and thought."

I called for prizes for inventions and new life for manufacturers and agriculture. I urged the creation of a city for manufacturers, which became Paterson, New Jersey. I demanded high ethical standards in government and set the stage for the modern civil service. I was the Father of the American government.

"The honor of a nation is its life."

When I took office, the United States was bankrupt. When I left office six years later, we were prosperous, with sound public credit, a stable government, and a working Constitution.

When my life in government and at George Washington's side ended, I was a poor man. My joy and wife, Eliza, and our eight children sacrificed for me. I sacrificed for my country.

"I am not worth exceeding $500 in the world. My slender fortune and the best years of my life have been devoted to the service of my adopted country."

I continued to fight for all people of every color and was a strong believer in merit as the foundation of success.

"I think the first duty of society is justice."

I championed the creation of a professional army and served as inspector general and a major general.

I assisted in founding the oldest surviving newspaper in America, the New York *Evening Post*.

I helped form two banks. I founded the Coast Guard.

I also made time for the outdoors, hunting with my special retriever, Old Peggy.

I enjoyed the theater, symphony, and walking the streets of my favorite young city, New York.

Mine was a life of enormous consequence that, by accident, I, an immigrant, could find in America a land that loved me as much as I loved her.

Author's Note

Alexander Hamilton was an unknown immigrant, an orphan, a boy of no connections and little promise who helped transform the world. At Washington's side, he helped bring victory to the American cause, wrote most of the Federalist Papers, and helped to create the prosperous colossus that is the United States. Sadly, on July 11, 1804, Hamilton was shot in a duel with Aaron Burr, the sitting vice president, on the New Jersey side of the Hudson River. Hamilton was carried back to New York City where he died. His legacy survives to this day.

Bibliography

Chernow, Ron. *Alexander Hamilton*. New York: Penguin Press, 2004.

Ellis, Joseph J. *The Quartet: Orchestrating the Second American Revolution, 1783–1789*. New York: Vintage, 2015.

Flexner, James Thomas. *Washington: The Indispensable Man*. New York: Back Bay Books, 1994.

Hamilton, Alexander, John Jay, and James Madison. *The Federalist Papers*. CreateSpace Independent Publishing Platform, 2019.

Randall, Willard Sterne. *Alexander Hamilton: A Life*. New York: Harper Collins, 2003.

Sylla, Richard. *Alexander Hamilton: The Illustrated Biography*. New York: Sterling Books, 2018.